Worship at the Keys
A Method Book

Donna Gielow McFarland

Also by Donna McFarland

Music Instruction
Follow the Star: Christmas Songs for Piano (Primer – Level 5)
Follow the Star: Christmas Songs for Piano Fake Book
Intro to Piano: Class Piano for Adult Beginners
Music Theory Made Simpl(er)
Intervals, Scales and Chords (oh, my!)

Kidlit
Duck and Friends: The Dinosaur Bones
Duck and Friends: The Computer Chase
The Purple Elephant
The Purple Elephant: The Journey Home
Sam and the Dragon: A Medieval Mars Story

Contributed Piano Arrangements to:
Hymns 'n Spirituals at Your Fingertips
Folk Songs 'n Favorites at Your Fingertips
Fast Track Solos

To God Be the Glory

(Cover photograph by Inna Vlasova)

Copyright © 2018 Donna Gielow McFarland
Illustrations copyright © 2017 Jack Foster

All rights reserved. No part of this book, including lead sheets and chord charts, may be reprinted in any manner whatsoever without written permission except in the case of brief quotations embodied in critical articles or reviews.
Reprinting of the letter to worship leaders is permitted.

Address inquiries to: spencermeadowpress@gmail.com
Visit our website at: www.duckandfriends.com

Published by Spencer Meadow Press

Printed in the U.S.A.
First Edition, April, 2018

Table of Contents

Acknowledgments..4
To the Student...5
To the Teacher..5
To Worship Leaders..7

Unit 1: Playing the Bass Line..................9
Keyboard Styles..9
Step 1: Lead Sheets and Chord Charts..............9
Step 2: Adding a Bass Line..............................10
Step 3: Worship Song Practice..........................11
Here I Am to Worship......................................12
This Is the Day..14
Theory Corner..15
Triads..15
New Chords: C, F, G..15
12-Bar Blues..16
Hunt 'n Peck (Learning to Play by Ear)..........17

Unit 2: Adding Right Hand Chords......18
Keyboard Styles..18
Step 1: Adding Triads......................................18
Step 2: Adding Triads in Rhythm......................19
Step 3: Worship Song Practice..........................19
He's Got the Whole World................................20
What a Beautiful Name....................................21
Cornerstone..22
Theory Corner..23
Inversions..23
Chord Progression..24
New Chords: Dm, Em, Am................................24
12-Bar Blues..24
Hunt 'n Peck..25

Unit 3: Using Inversions........................26
Keyboard Styles..26
Step 1: Adding Inversions................................26
Step 2: Triad Inversions with Bass Line............27
Step 3: Worship Song Practice..........................27
Jesus Paid It All..28
Lord, I Need You..29
Amazing Grace (My Chains Are Gone)..30
Theory Corner..31
Diatonic Chords..31
Inversion Practice..32
Diatonic Chord Progressions............................32
"Heart and Soul" Chord Progression................32
Hunt 'n Peck..33

Unit 4: Adding Bass Line Rhythms......34
Keyboard Styles..34
Step 1: Adding Rhythm to the Bass Line..................34
Step 2: Hands Together with Rhythmic Bass Line...35
Step 3: Worship Song Practice..........................35
Holy Spirit..36
At the Cross (Love Ran Red)..................37
From the Inside Out......................................38
Theory Corner..40
Diatonic Chords in G Major..............................40
New Chords: D, Bm..40
Transposing..41
"Heart and Soul" Chord Progression in G............41
Hunt 'n Peck..42

Unit 5: Playing Chord Charts................43
Keyboard Styles..43
Step 1: Lead Sheets and Chord Charts............43
Step 2: Adding More Notes to the Bass Line......44
Step 3: Worship Song Practice..........................45
Breathe..45
You Never Let Go..46
Every Move I Make..47
Happy Day..48
Theory Corner..49
Major and Minor Triads....................................49
New Chords: Cm, Fm, Gm................................50
12-Bar Blues..50
Hunt 'n Peck..51

Unit 6: Flexibility....................................52
Keyboard Styles..52
Step 1: Playing with a Worship Team..............52
Step 2: Practicing Being Flexible......................54
Step 3: Worship Song Practice..........................54
10,000 Reasons..55
My All in All..56
Your Love Awakens Me....................................57
Theory Corner..58
Major and Minor Triads....................................58
Chords with Numbers......................................59
Sus Chords..59
Diminished and Augmented Chords..................60
Using New Chords..60
Jesus, Lover of My Soul..................................60
Hunt 'n Peck..61

Unit 7: Playing in New Keys..................**62**
   Keyboard Styles..62
      Step 1: Learning Songs in a New Key: D.................62
      Step 2: Practice Chord Progressions.....................62
      Step 3: Worship Song Practice..............................63
   Our God..63
   Open the Eyes of My Heart....................64
   You Are My King (Amazing Love).........65

   Oceans (Where Feet May Fail)...............66
   Theory Corner..67
      Transposing..67
      Improvising in D..68
   Hunt 'n Peck..69
Chart of Chords.....................................**70**
Transposition Chart............................**72**

ACKNOWLEDGMENTS

A publication like this would not be possible without the contributions of many people. Cherry Wilson and Tami Wilson provided invaluable assistance by reviewing content as the manuscript progressed, along with editing and proofreading. In addition to their work on the manuscript, their constant encouragement kept me on track.

I'd also like to thank Jennifer Searle, Kristy Parks, Pamela Vining, Matt Eerdman, Levi Bagge, Evan Phan and the worship teams at Eugene First Baptist Church for their contributions to my research and for their inspiration and encouragement.

Thank you to Jack Foster for catching the vision with his musical chickens.

I express my gratitude to Dr. Richard Clarke and Dr. Ed Kammerer, my music professors at the University of Oregon, and also pastor Gene Skinner. They guided me in researching and writing my masters' project, which dealt with teaching classically trained pianists to play piano for evangelical church services.

My husband, Scott, helped with the cover. Thank you!

My parents provided years of piano lessons, listening to me practice for hours and hours. Then they put me through college and grad school in music.

And finally, thanks be to God. May this book be used in His service and for His glory.

To the Student

Do you want to play piano or keyboard with a church worship team? This book is for you! You can learn how to play songs from chord charts and lead sheets. If you have taken a few years of piano lessons then you are ready to get started. Although you can use this book on your own, it will be helpful to work with a teacher. You also need lots of patience. It can take a while to learn how to play "the keys" for worship. The first song takes the longest, but then it gets easier and easier. And if you keep going, someday you'll be so quick you can sightread new songs.

If you already play in a band or if you've been asked to join a worship team, feel free to make a copy of the letter on page 7 "To Worship Leaders" and give it to your worship team leader.

May God bless you as you use your skills to worship Him!

To the Teacher

Do you have a piano student who wants to play in a middle school or high school church worship band? Often a youth pastor will learn that a student in the youth group plays piano and they will invite the student to play keyboard with the worship team. The student is given copies of songs, probably in chord chart form (only words and chord symbols), without any idea of what to do with them. This book can help.

Contained in this book is a step-by-step method, paced for teens, for how to get started playing worship lead sheets and chord charts. Each unit contains three sections: Keyboard Styles (what to do with the songs), Theory Corner (the concepts and chords needed for the next unit's Keyboard Styles section) and Hunt 'n Peck (playing by ear). Much of what the student will be playing as they advance beyond this book will require good ear skills, and the Hunt 'n Peck sections help the student develop these skills.

This method is designed for students who have already studied piano for a few years. It assumes that the student can play hands together, read treble and bass clefs, and has at least a rudimentary understanding of key signatures and time signatures.

If you are using this book with a student who is already playing in a band, you may want to pre-read Unit 6, which is particularly relevant to playing with other musicians. It also explains how to simplify the complicated chords your student may encounter.

I hope you and your student find it helpful!

Donna McFarland

TO WORSHIP LEADERS

You are receiving this letter because you have invited a middle school or high school student to play keyboard with your worship team. Thank you! Thank you! Thank you! Your willingness to include students in your band will pay off as you provide learning opportunities for the next generation of worship leaders.

If you are not a keyboard player yourself, there are some things that are helpful to know. Your student has probably taken several years of piano lessons, but that may not have prepared them to play worship songs. There is a steep learning curve for a traditional piano student to learn how to play from chord charts and lead sheets. Most piano students are also not used to playing with others and at first it may be challenging for them to keep up. What this means is that when the student first joins your worship team, they might not be very good. However, if you give them opportunities to play, you will see amazing progress, hopefully leading to a very competent worship keyboardist.

There are some things you can do to help make their learning process quicker and easier:

- Give lots of lead time to learn new songs – at least a week, more is better. Later, they will be able to learn songs with one day notice. Eventually, they will be able to sightread new songs. It might be a very long time before they can play by ear.

- Consider having your new keys player start by playing only one or two songs, or play only for rehearsals. Soon they will be ready to participate more fully.

- To ease the learning curve, if possible provide both lead sheets (music, chords and lyrics) and chord charts (chords and lyrics). If you want your student to play the melody they will definitely need a lead sheet. If your church is a member of CCLI, you should be able to print any lead sheet or chord chart in any key.

- Don't ask your student to transpose – give them songs in the keys you plan to use.

- Provide a music stand so they can easily see their music.

- If you want something specific, talk to your keys player about what parts you need them to play (bass line? chords? melody?). They probably won't be able to do anything fancy for a while.

- Offer lots of encouragement, especially at first. Your student is working hard!

Thank you for having the vision to include students on your worship team. May God bless you!

Donna McFarland
author of *Worship at the Keys: A Method Book*

Unit 1: Playing the Bass Line

KEYBOARD STYLES

Step 1: Lead Sheets and Chord Charts

Worship songs usually come in two formats. Here is a lead sheet. It shows the melody (the music), the words and the chord symbols (C, G, F).

"Here I Am to Worship (Light of the World)" by Tim Hughes
Copyright © 2001 Thankyou Music (PRS) (adm. worldwide at CapitolCMGPublishing.com excluding Europe which is adm. by Integrity Music, part of the David C Cook family. Songs@integrigymusic.com) All rights reserved. Used by permission.

Here is a chord chart. Chord charts show only words and chord symbols.

```
             C              G
Here I am to worship, Here I am to bow down,

             C              F
Here I am to say that You're my God.

                  C              G
You're altogether lovely, Altogether worthy,

             C         F
Altogether wonderful to me.
```

Worship at the Keys: A Method Book

Step 2: Adding a Bass Line

Let's start with lead sheets. You can use the chord symbols to make a bass line. If the chord symbol is **C**, play a "C" in the bass. If the chord symbol is **G**, play a "G". As you practice the bass line, you may either sing the melody or play it with your right hand. Look at the bass line in the example below:

Play the bass note on beat one even if the melody does something different, like in the second measure below:

Sometimes the chord symbol has two parts like this: **G/B**. Play the last letter, a "B," in the bass.

Step 3: Worship Song Practice

When leading worship, it is important to keep a steady beat. As you practice, play slowly enough that you can continue without hesitating. Practice with a metronome if it helps.

When you make a mistake (everybody does sometimes!), just keep playing as though your note was correct. If you don't stop, the singers and band members will probably not even notice that you made a mistake. If you stop, they'll notice.

Here is the chorus for *Here I Am to Worship*. Play the bass line with your left hand and either sing (or hum) the melody or play the melody with your right hand.

"Here I Am to Worship (Light of the World)" by Tim Hughes
Copyright © 2001 Thankyou Music (PRS) (adm. worldwide at CapitolCMGPublishing.com excluding Europe which is adm. by Integrity Music, part of the David C Cook family. Songs@integrigymusic.com) All rights reserved. Used by permission.

Worship at the Keys: A Method Book

Here is the full lead sheet for *Here I Am to Worship*. When you see a Dm chord symbol, play "D" in your left hand. If there is a measure with no chord symbol it means that the chord from the previous measure is continuing. Replay the bass note on beat one of the new measure. Remember to keep a steady beat.

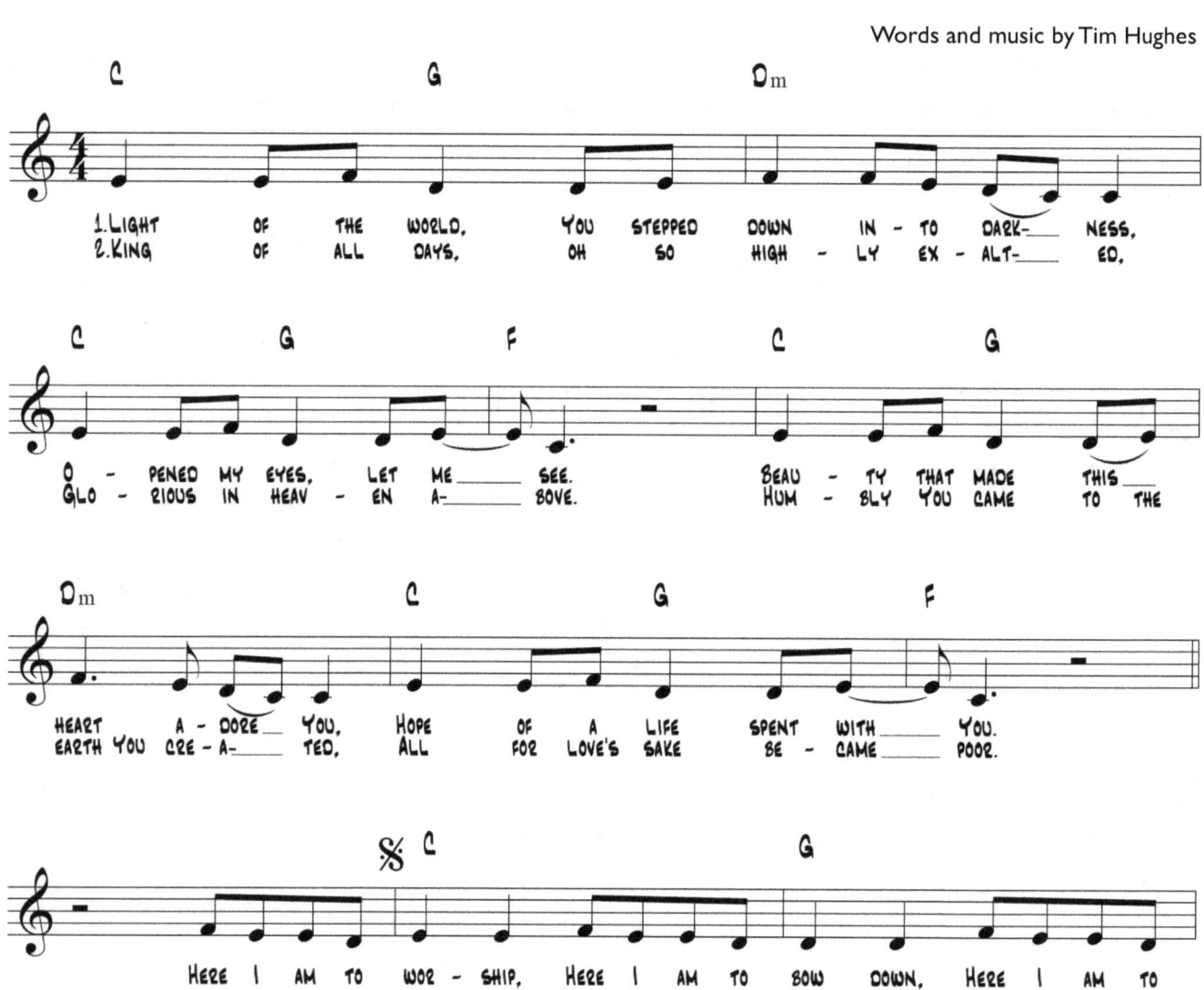

Copyright © 2001 Thankyou Music (PRS) (adm. worldwide at CapitolCMGPublishing.com excluding Europe which is adm. by Integrity Music, part of the David C Cook family. Songs@integritymusic.com) All rights reserved. Used by permission.

Here is another lead sheet. Play the bass line using the same method as *Here I Am to Worship*. On measures with no chord symbol, replay the bass note from the previous measure.

Copyright © 1967 Universal Music – Brentwood Benson Publ. (ASCAP) (adm. at CapitolCMGPublishing.com)
All rights reserved. Used by permission.

THEORY CORNER

Triads

Triads are chords made up of three notes. They look like this:

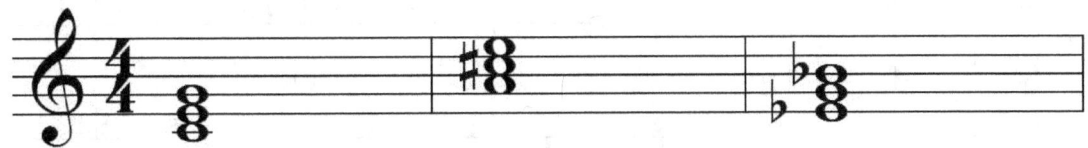

Triads have a root, a third and a fifth.

Chords are named by the root – if the root is C then the chord is a C chord. A capital C means that the chord is a C major triad. "Cm" represents a C minor triad (more about minor later). "C7" is another type of C chord which has four notes. There is a chart in the back of this book that shows more types of chords.

New Chords: C, F, G

You can start with only three chords. Here are the C, F and G major triads. These triads are written in what is called "root position" because the root is the lowest note.

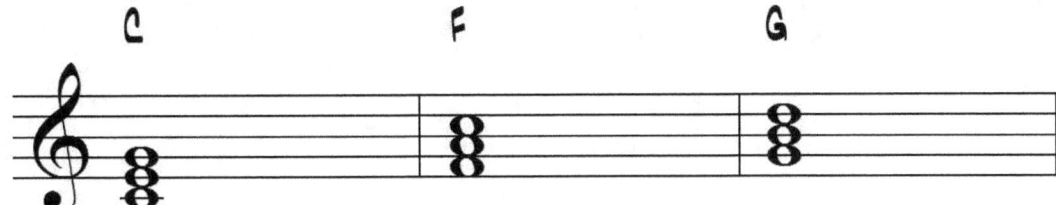

Worship at the Keys: A Method Book

In order to play worship lead sheets and chord charts, you will need to learn how to play chords. Practice playing these major triads with your right hand and the bass note in your left hand. Keep a steady beat as you play.

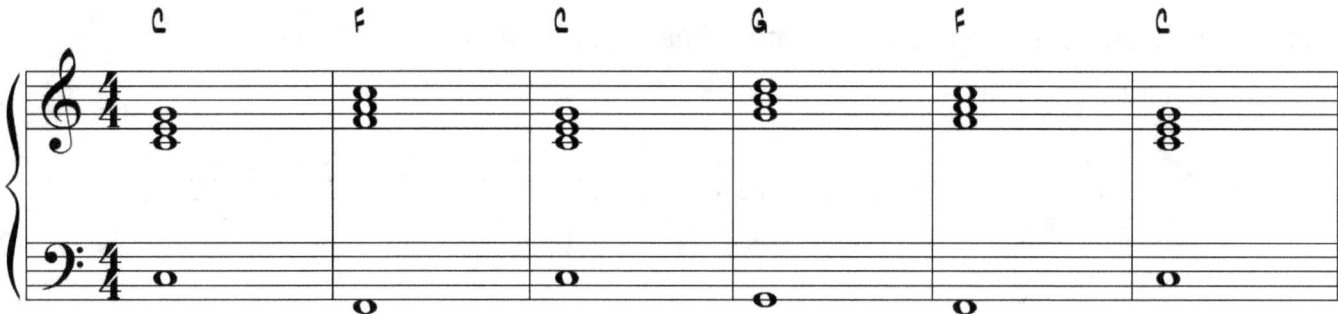

12-Bar Blues

You can have some fun with just three chords. Here is a pattern for the 12-bar blues. Each chord gets four beats, so play four measures of a C major triad, two measures of F major, etc. After you are comfortable playing the chords as whole notes, try adding your own rhythm in your right or left hand.

12-Bar Blues Pattern #1

C	C	C	C
F	F	C	C
G	F	C	C

HUNT 'N PECK (LEARNING TO PLAY BY EAR)

The better you can play by ear, the more fun it will be to improvise on the piano. You can start by figuring out how to play some familiar songs using just the black keys!

The following songs can be played using ONLY black keys. Choose songs you recognize and start on the given note. Work at it until you can play each melody. Don't worry about fingering, just move around if you need to.

Rain, Rain, Go Away (start on F#)

Old MacDonald Had a Farm (start on F#)

Amazing Grace (start on C#)

Swing Low (start on Bb)

Auld Lang Syne (start on C# – you might need one white key)

Worship at the Keys: A Method Book

Unit 2: Adding Right Hand Chords

KEYBOARD STYLES

Step 1: Adding Triads

Now that you can play a bass line, it's time to add chords in your right hand. We will start with the root position triads you already know. Here are the first two lines of *Here I Am to Worship*.

"Here I Am to Worship (Light of the World)" by Tim Hughes
Copyright © 2001 Thankyou Music (PRS) (adm. worldwide at CapitolCMGPublishing.com excluding Europe which is adm. by Integrity Music, part of the David C Cook family. Songs@integrigymusic.com) All rights reserved. Used by permission.

And here is what you would play if you use root position triads in your right hand and the bass line in your left hand.

Step 2: Adding Triads in Rhythm

Once you are comfortable playing triads as whole notes, you are ready to add some rhythm. Keep it simple. Play the triads as quarter notes, regardless of what happens in the rhythm of the melody. Remember to keep a steady beat.

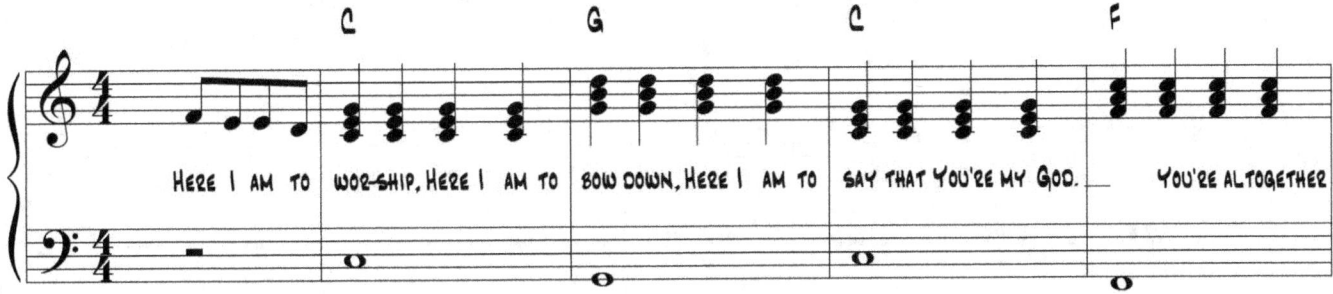

Step 3: Worship Song Practice

Use the quarter-note rhythm on the chorus of *Here I Am to Worship*. Play slowly enough that you can keep the rhythm steady and keep going even if you make a mistake.

Worship at the Keys: A Method Book

Practice these lead sheets with whole-note or quarter-note triads in your right hand and a bass line in your left hand.

He's Got the Whole World

American Spiritual

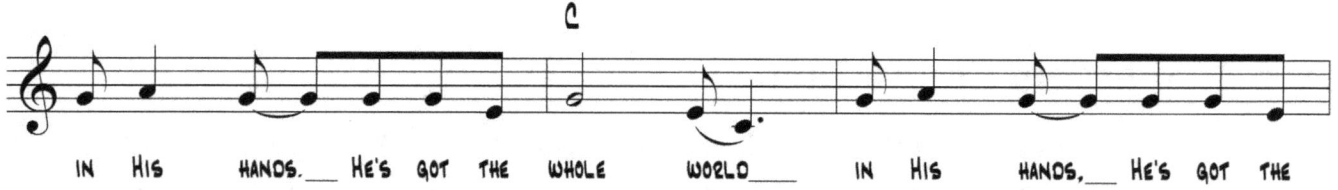

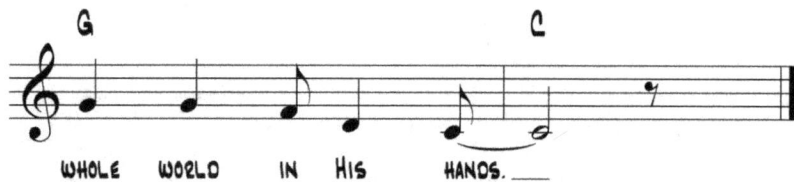

The next two lead sheets use C, F, G and Am. Here is the Am triad: Play an "A" in the bass and the Am triad in your right hand.

G/B is called a "slash" chord. Play a G triad in your right hand and a "B" in your left hand.

20 Unit 2: Adding Right Hand Chords

Sometimes there is a rest in the melody on the first beat of the measure. Play the right hand chord and bass note on beat one anyway. Leave the complicated rhythms to the singers – just play quarter-note triads in your right hand.

Copyright © 2016 Hillsong Music Publishing (APRA) (adm. in the US and Canada at CapitolCMGPublishing.com) All rights reserved. Used by permission.

Cornerstone

Words and music by
Edward Mote, Eric Liljero, Jonas Myrin and Reuben Morgan

My hope is built on noth-ing less than Je-sus' blood and right-eous-ness.

I dare not trust the sweet-est frame, but whol-ly trust in Je-sus' name.

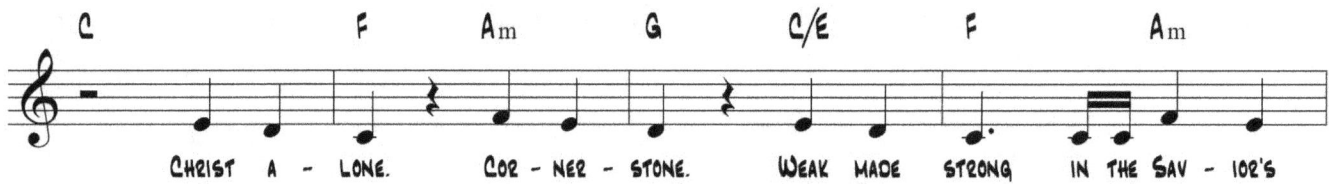
Christ a-lone. Cor-ner-stone. Weak made strong in the Sav-ior's

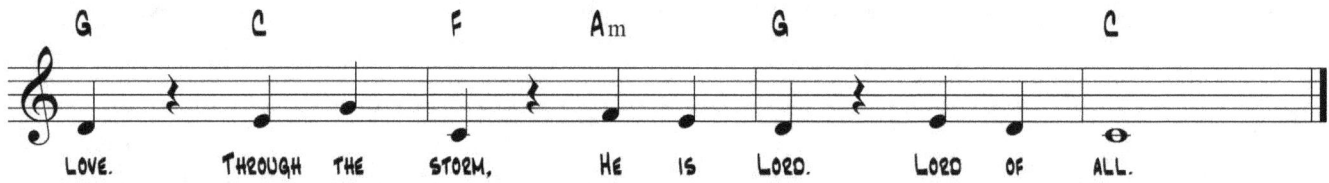
love. Through the storm, He is Lord. Lord of all.

Copyright © 2012 Hillsong Music Publishing (APRA) (adm. in the US and Canada at CapitolCMGPublishing.com)
All rights reserved. Used by permission.

THEORY CORNER

Inversions

The C major triad contains the notes "C," "E" and "G." These three notes can be played in any order and will still be a C major triad. When the "C" is the lowest note, the triad is in root position. When one of the other notes is the lowest note, the triad is in an inversion.

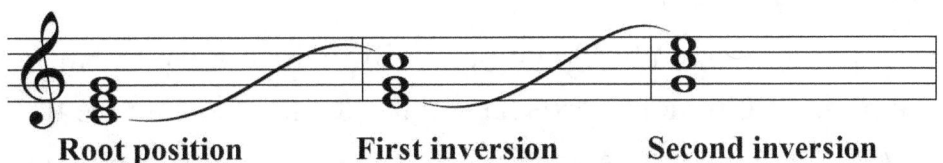

Root position   First inversion   Second inversion

Play these two examples. Which one sounds smoother?

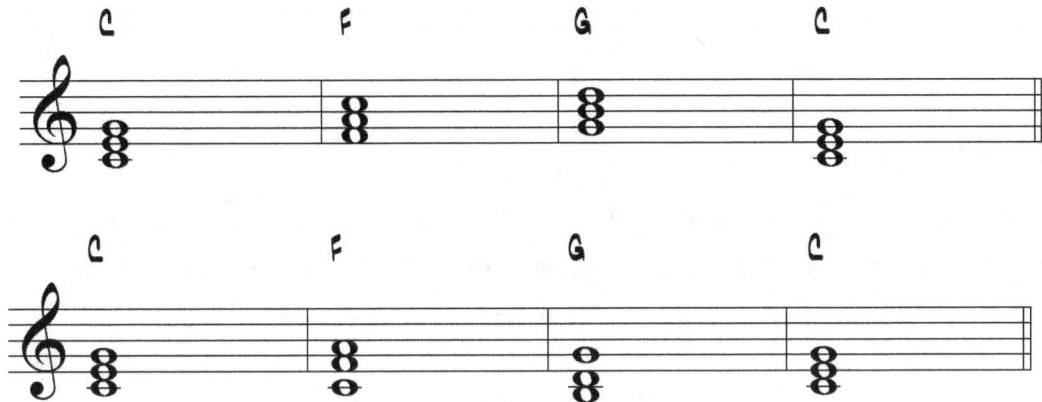

To practice inversions, choose a chord and go up and down the keyboard with your right hand finding and playing the inversions. Practice the F major triad like this:

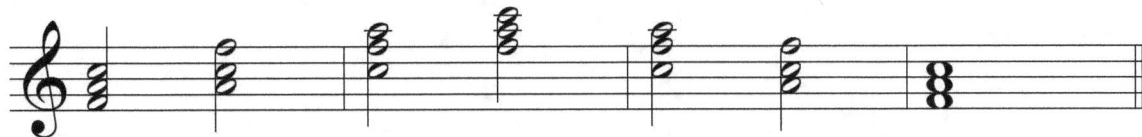

Once you have learned the inversions for F major, challenge yourself to play the chord with "F" as the highest note. Then "A" as the highest note. Then "C" as the highest note. Practice the C major and G major triad inversions the same way.

Worship at the Keys: A Method Book

Chord Progression

Now it is time to try a series of chords (a chord progression) using inversions. For the chord progression below, start with the C chord in root position. Work out how to play the rest of the chords in root position or inversions so they sound smooth.

C   F   C   G   C

New Chords: Dm, Em, Am

These chords are minor, so the chord symbols will include a small "m." Unlike major chords which sound bright, minor chords have a darker sound. Practice these new chords in root position. Also practice inversions for Am because you will need them in Unit 3.

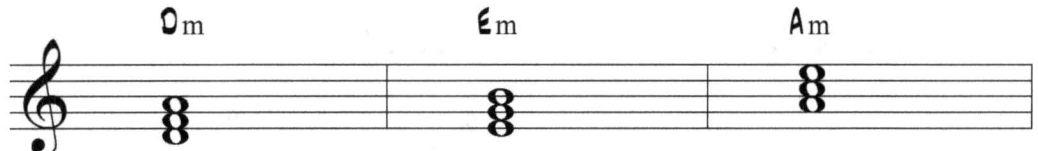

12-Bar Blues

With more chords, the 12-bar blues pattern becomes even more interesting. Remember, each chord gets four beats. You can play these chords in root position or inversions. Try adding your own rhythm in your right or left hand. Make sure to keep a steady beat!

12-Bar Blues Pattern #2

C	F	C	C
F	F	C	C
Dm	G	C	C

HUNT 'N PECK

You can play some melodies by ear using only white keys. Choose as many of these songs as you recognize and figure out how to play them, starting on the given note.

Mary Had a Little Lamb (start on E)

London Bridge is Falling Down (start on G)

Yankee Doodle (start on C)

Alouette (start on C)

The Alphabet Song/Twinkle, Twinkle Little Star (start on C)

Worship at the Keys: A Method Book

Unit 3: Using Inversions

KEYBOARD STYLES

Step 1: Adding Inversions

It's time to smooth out the chords in your right hand by using some inversions. Look at this section of *Jesus Paid It All*.

"Jesus Paid it All" by Alex Nifong
Copyright © 2006 worshiptogether.com Songs (ASCAP) sixsteps Music (ASCAP) Pay Me Please Publishing (ASCAP) (adm. at CapitolCMGPublishing.com) All rights reserved. Used by permission.

You could play these triads in root position, but it will sound better to use some inversions. Play each line below. Which sounds smoother?

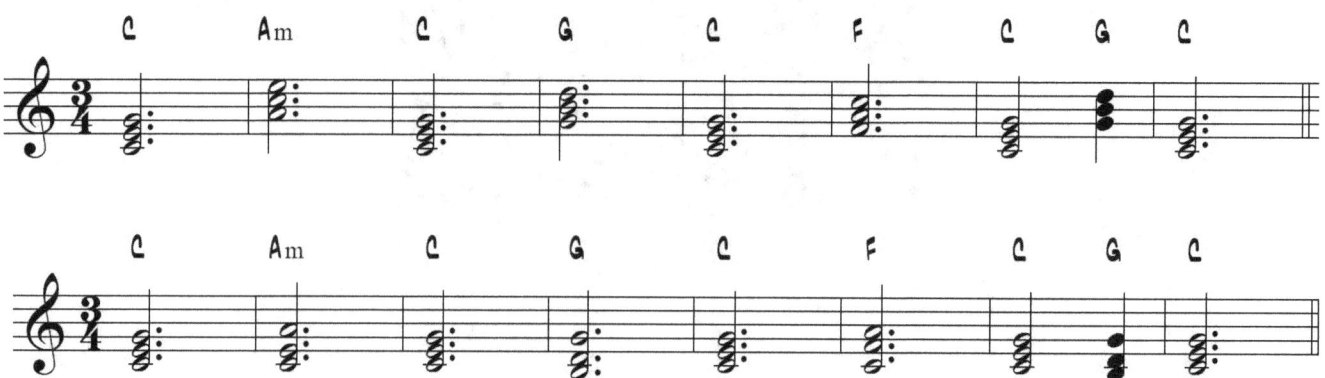

Step 2: Triad Inversions with Bass Line

When you begin a new lead sheet, practice the right hand chords until you can play them smoothly using at least some inversions. You can play long notes or play a quarter note rhythm. Add in the bass line when you are ready. Here is an example of how you could play the chorus to *Jesus Paid It All*.

Step 3: Worship Song Practice

The lead sheets on the following pages can all be played with right hand chords in root position and inversions (quarter-note or whole-note rhythms) and a bass line. Play slowly enough that you can keep a steady beat.

Worship at the Keys: A Method Book

Jesus Paid It All

Words and music by Alex Nifong

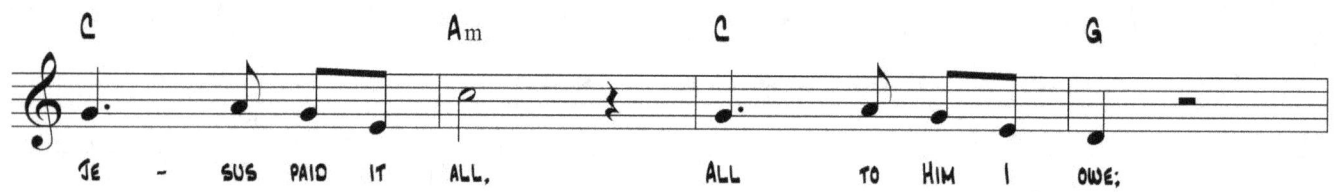

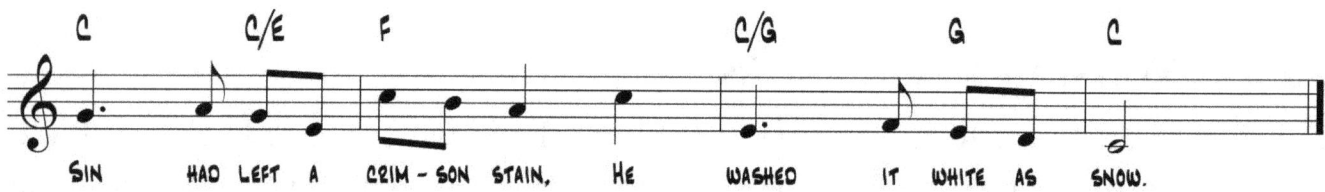

Copyright © 2006 worshiptogether.com Songs (ASCAP) sixsteps Music (ASCAP) Pay Me Please Publishing (ASCAP) (adm. at CapitolCMGPublishing.com) All rights reserved. Used by permission.

Lord, I Need You

Words and music by
Christy Nockels, Daniel Carson, Jesse Reeves, Kristian Stanfill and Matt Maher

Copyright © 2011 Thankyou Music (PRS) (adm. worldwide at CapitolCMGPublishing.com excluding Europe which is adm. by Integrity Music, part of the David C Cook family. Songs@integritymusic.com)/worshiptogether.com Songs (ASCAP) sixsteps Music (ASCAP) Sweater Weather Music (ASCAP) Valley of Songs Music (BMI) (adm. at CapitolCMGPublishing.com) All rights reserved. Used by permission.

Worship at the Keys: A Method Book

This song uses the Dm triad. You can play it in root position.

Amazing Grace (My Chains Are Gone)

Words and music by Chris Tomlin and Louie Giglio

A-maz-ing grace, how sweet the sound that saved a wretch like me. I once was lost, but now I'm found, was blind but now I see. My chains are gone. I've been set free. My God my Sav-ior has ran-somed me. And like a flood, His mer-cy reigns, un-end-ing love, a-maz-ing grace.

Copyright © 2006 worshiptogether.com Songs (ASCAP) sixsteps Music (ASCAP) Vamos Publishing (ASCAP) (adm. at CapitolCMGPublishing.com) All rights reserved. Used by permission.

THEORY CORNER

Diatonic Chords

Everybody likes the key of C – it's all white keys! "Diatonic" chords use only notes in the scale, so diatonic chords in C major use only white keys. Here is the C major scale with the scale degrees (the notes in the scale) numbered:

Here are the chords you have learned so far. They are diatonic chords in C. Notice they only use white keys.

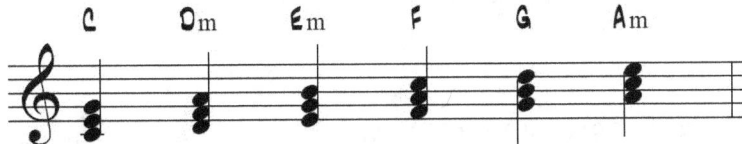

The triads built on scale degrees 1, 4 and 5 are major and the triads built on scale degrees 2, 3 and 6 are minor. This will be true for diatonic triads in any major key.

Sometimes scale degree numbers are written with Roman numerals. The Roman numeral represents the whole triad built on that scale degree. An uppercase Roman numeral means the chord is major and lowercase means minor. The "C:" means the key of C major.

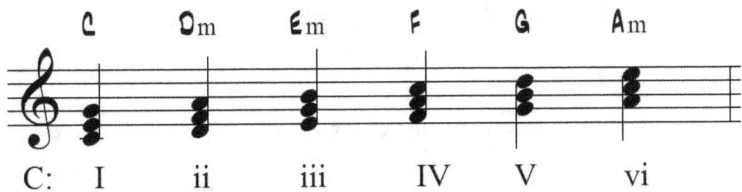

You might wonder why there is no triad on B. There is, but the triad built on B is not major or minor – it is diminished and we won't be using it in this book. It is listed in the chart of chords in the back, though, if you are curious.

Worship at the Keys: A Method Book

Inversion Practice

It might take some time before you can use chord inversions without having to work hard. Continue practicing the inversions of C, F, G and Am triads and add inversion practice for Dm and Em.

Diatonic Chord Progressions

Here is the chord progression you learned in Unit 2 along with a new chord progression. Both use diatonic chords in C. Practice until you can play the chords smoothly using some inversions. Start with the first chord in root position. Figure out the smoothest way to play the chord progression. Then try it again starting with the first chord in an inversion. Play the bass line with your left hand.

Chord Progression #1: C   F   C   G   C

Chord Progression #2: Em   Am   Dm   G   C

"Heart and Soul" Chord Progression

Another chord progression that uses all diatonic chords is the lower part of the duet, *Heart and Soul*. Here is the chord progression:

C   Am   F   G   (repeat)

Try playing the *Heart and Soul* chord progression different ways. Play chords in your right hand using triads in root position and inversions. Add the bass line and try out different rhythmic patterns. Once you have invented some variations, find a friend to play the melody. Tell your mom you're practicing.

Hunt 'n Peck

Here are some melodies to play by ear. This time you will need to figure out for yourself what note to start on. Before you play each tune, play one of the chord progressions from the previous page. Which note sounds like the right starting note?

Row, Row, Row Your Boat

Pop! Goes the Weasel

Jingle Bells

Kum-Ba-Yah

Joy to the World!

Worship at the Keys: A Method Book

Unit 4: Adding Bass Line Rhythms

KEYBOARD STYLES

Step 1: Adding Rhythm to the Bass Line

Now we'll add some rhythm to the bass line. Many worship keyboardists like to repeat the bass notes using a dotted rhythm. This fills in the sound and adds more flow to their playing. Bass notes can also be played in other octaves.

A bass line for *Holy Spirit* could look something like this:

Notice that the rhythm in the bass line varies – not every measure is exactly the same. Look at the second line of this song and write in a possible bass line.

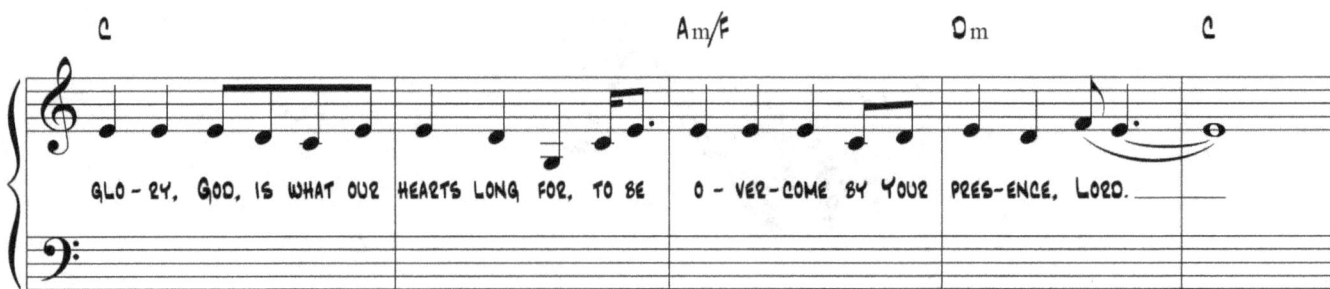

Step 2: Hands Together with Rhythmic Bass Line

The next step is to play the lead sheet using triads in root position and inversions in a steady quarter-note rhythm, while adding some rhythmic interest to the bass line. (You can play whole notes in your right hand if quarter notes feel too complicated right now.)

Holy Spirit could sound like the example below. For the Am/F chord, play an Am triad in your right hand and an "F" in the bass.

Step 3: Worship Song Practice

Practice the lead sheet below and the songs on the following pages with triads in your right hand, while adding some rhythm to the bass line in your left hand. Use the pedal if you are not doing so already.

Worship at the Keys: A Method Book

Holy Spirit

Words and music by
Bryan Torwalt and Katie Torwalt

Copyright © 2011 Capitol CMG Genesis (ASCAP) Jesus Culture Music (ASCAP) (adm. at CapitolCMGPublishing.com)
All rights reserved. Used by permission.

At the Cross (Love Ran Red)

Words and music by
Chris Tomlin, Ed Cash, Jonas Myrin, Matt Armstrong and Matt Redman

Copyright © 2014 Thankyou Music (PRS) (adm. worldwide at CapitolCMGPublishing.com excluding Europe which is adm. by Integrity Music, part of the David C Cook family. Songs@integritymusic.com) / Atlas Mountain Songs (BMI) worshiptogether.com Songs (ASCAP) S.D.G. Publishing (BMI) Universal Music – Brentwood Benson Songs (BMI) Universal Music – Brentwood Benson Tunes (SESAC) Countless Wonder Publishing (SESAC) Fots Music (SESAC) McKittrick Music (BMI) (adm. at CapitolCMGPublishing.com) All rights reserved. Used by permission.

Worship at the Keys: A Method Book

Theory Corner

Diatonic Chords in G Major

The key of G major has one sharp in the key signature. Here is the G major scale:

Most of the diatonic chords in G major are the same chords we saw in C major, but they land on different scale degrees than they did in the key of C.

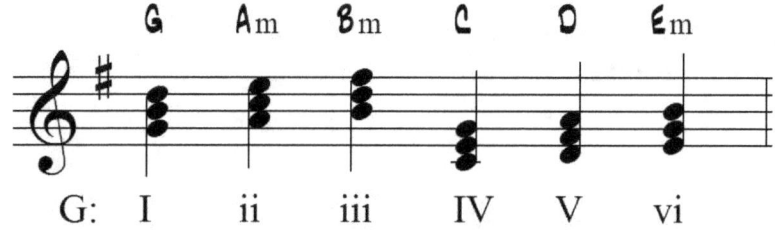

New Chords: D, Bm

There are two new chords that are diatonic to the key of G. They are D and Bm. These chords use F# because there is an F# in the key signature for the G major scale. Practice these chords in root position and inversions.

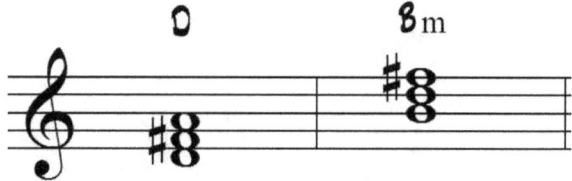

Transposing

There may be times that you need to take a song in one key and play it in another key. This is called transposing. Roman numerals can help you do this. Look at the chart:

Key	Key Sig.	I	ii	iii	IV	V	vi
C	nothing	C	Dm	Em	F	G	Am
G	F#	G	Am	Bm	C	D	Em

Suppose you have this chord progression in C major:

      Em   Am   Dm   G   C

but you want to play it in G major. Look at the chart above and choose the chords in G that are under the chords in C. Your new chord progression is:

      Bm   Em   Am   D   G

Practice each of these chord progressions and hear how they sound alike.

"Heart and Soul" Chord Progression in G

This is the chord progression from *Heart and Soul* that you played in Unit 3. It is in the key of C.

      C   Am   F   G

Transpose this chord progression to the key of G. You can write the chord symbols here:

Now practice the progression from *Heart and Soul* in the key of G.

Worship at the Keys: A Method Book

Hunt 'n Peck

Here are some melodies to play by ear. The starting notes given for these songs are for the key of G major. Remember that the G major scale uses F#. Before you play each song, play one of these chord progressions:

    Chord progression #1:   G   C   G   D   G

    Chord progression #2:   Bm   Em   Am   D   G

- Brother John (Are You Sleeping?) (start on G)
- I Love You, Lord (start on D)
- Happy Birthday to You (start on D)
- My Country 'Tis of Thee (start on G)
- Heart & Soul (start on G)

Now that you've played the songs in G, you can play the **C-F-C-G-C** chord progression and play them again, this time in the key of C. You'll have to find a new starting note for each song.

Unit 4: Adding Bass Line Rhythms

Unit 5: Playing Chord Charts

KEYBOARD STYLES

Step 1: Lead Sheets and Chord Charts

Here is a section of the lead sheet for *Breathe*. It's in the key of G major.

"Breathe" by Marie Barnett
© 1995 Mercy/Vineyard Publishing (ASCAP) Admin. in North America by Music Services o/b/o Vineyard Music USA
All rights reserved. Used by permission.

Here is *Breathe* as a chord chart:

```
   G            C/G          G            C/G
   This is the air I breathe.    This is the air I breathe.

   G  D/F#  Em    D         C    Em    D
   Your holy presence       living    in me.
```

Worship at the Keys: A Method Book

The lead sheet and the chord chart both show the same chords, but there is nothing in the chord chart that tells you how many beats to play each chord, so you have to use your ear to know when to change the chord. If you only have a chord chart and you haven't heard the song before, find a recording or YouTube video and listen until the song is familiar to you. Usually chords last for either two or four beats before they change.

From the lead sheet or the chord chart, *Breathe* could start like this:

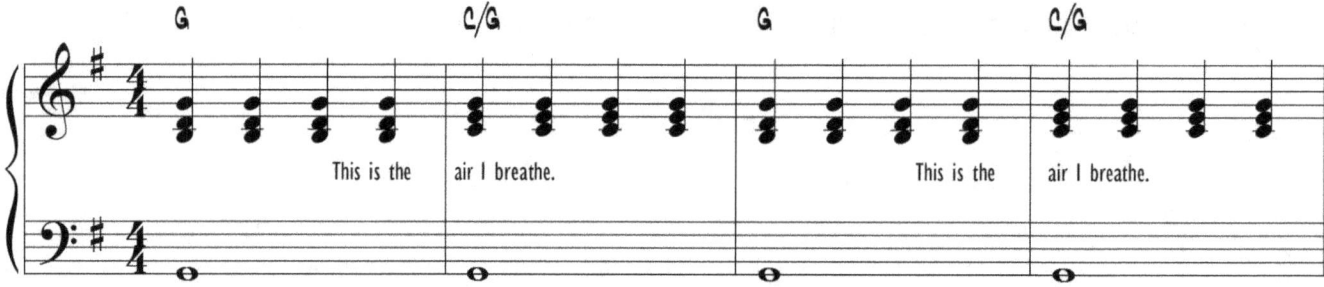

Step 2: Adding More Notes to the Bass Line

While playing steady quarter notes in your right hand, you can make the bass line more interesting by adding dotted-note rhythms and changing octaves. You can even add notes that connect one bass note to another. Look at this example from the second line of the song:

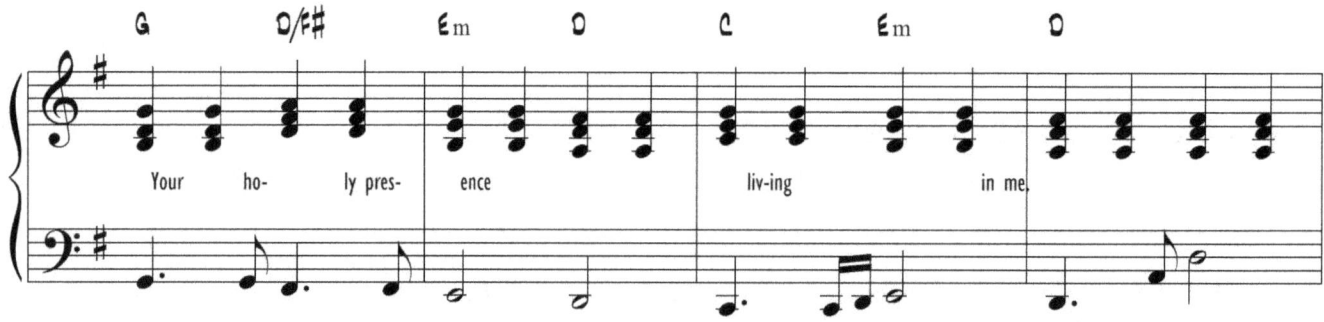

If this step feels too complicated right now, just look it over and move on to Step 3. This technique is normally used only when you're playing solo or in a band without a bass player.

Step 3: Worship Song Practice

Play *Breathe* and the songs on the next few pages using chord charts. Listen to a recording if you don't know the song or if you need to know where the chords change. You won't be able to play along with the recording unless it happens to be in the same key as your music, but it is still helpful to listen. For *Breathe*, use the examples in Steps 1 and 2 to get started.

Breathe

Words and Music by
Marie Barnett

```
G            C/G              G            C/G
 This is the air I breathe.    This is the air I breathe.

G   D/F#  Em    D     C    Em    D
 Your holy presence     living    in me.

G            C/G              G            C/G
 This is my daily bread.    This is my daily bread.

G   D/F#  Em    D     C    Em    D
 Your very  word       spoken   to me.

        G  D/F#  Em   D         C    Em   D
 And I                 I'm desperate for You.

        G  D/F#  Em   D         C    Em   D
 And I                 I'm lost without You.
```

© 1995 Mercy/Vineyard Publishing (ASCAP) Admin. in North America by Music Services o/b/o Vineyard Music USA
All rights reserved. Used by permission.

You Never Let Go

Words and music by
Beth Redman and Matt Redman

Verse

     G
Even though I walk through the valley of the shadow of death,

   C/E
Your perfect love is casting out fear.

      G
And even when I'm caught in the middle of the storms of this life,

 C/E
I won't turn back, I know You are near.

Pre-Chorus

     Em D G   Em D G
And I will fear no evil,   For my God is with me.

     Em D G
And if my God is with me

     D   C
Whom shall I fear? Whom shall I fear?

Chorus
G
Oh no, You never let go, through the calm and through the storm.

Em
Oh no, You never let go, in every high and every low.

D   C   G
Oh no, You never let go, Lord, You never let go of me.

Copyright © 2005 Thankyou Music (PRS) (adm. worldwide at CapitolCMGPublishing.com excluding Europe which is adm. by Integrity Music, part of the David C cook family. Songs@integritymusic.com) All rights reserved. Used by permission.

Every Move I Make

Words and music by
David Ruis

```
G              C           D            C
Ev'ry move I make, I make in You;   You make me move, Jesus.

G              C           D       C
Ev'ry breath I take I breathe in You.

G              C           D            C
Ev'ry step I take, I take in You;   You are my way, Jesus,

G              C           D     C
Ev'ry breath I take I take in You.


G          C        D      C
Waves of mercy, waves of grace,

G          C       D     C    G
Everywhere I look I see Your face.

        C         D     C
Your love has captured me,

G       C      D      C    G   C    D   C
Oh my God, this love how can it be.


G          C        D      C                (G)
La-la-la-la-la-la,  La-la-la-la-la-la  (repeat)
```

© 1996 Mercy/Vineyard Publishing (ASCAP) & Vineyard Songs (Canada) (SOCAN) Admin. in North America by Music Services o/b/o Vineyard Music USA. All rights reserved. Used by permission.

Happy Day

Words and music by
Ben Cantelon and Tim Hughes

C
The greatest day in history,

F
Death is beaten, You have rescued me.

Am   F
Sing it out, Jesus is alive!

C
The empty cross, the empty grave,

F
Life eternal, You have won the day,

Am   F
Shout it out, Jesus is alive!

C   F   Am   G
Oh, happy day, happy day, You washed my sin away.

C   F   Am   G   C F Am G
Oh happy day, happy day, I'll never be the same.

                 C   F Am G (C)
Forever I am changed.

Copyright © 2006 Thankyou Music (PRS) (adm. worldwide at CapitolCMGPublishing.com excluding Europe which is adm. by Integrity Music, part of the David C Cook family. Songs@integritymusic.com) All rights reserved. Used by permission.

THEORY CORNER

Major and Minor Triads

Lead sheets and chord charts use both major and minor triads. Compare the two triads below. What is different?

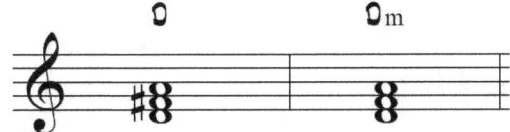

Remember, triads have a root, a third and a fifth. The third is the middle note when the triad is in root position. Even if the triad is in an inversion, the third doesn't change. In the example below, the third is F#. When a D major triad is played in an inversion, the third is still F#.

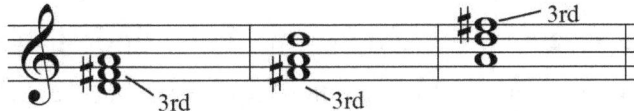

In order to change a major triad into a minor triad, lower the third of the triad by one half step (HS). A half step is the distance from one piano key to the very next key, regardless of color. For example:

Look at the D and Dm triads and you can see that the third is one half step lower in Dm.

On the staff below are three major triads. Next to each major triad, write the minor triad by rewriting the chord with the third one half step lower. You can check your work on the next page.

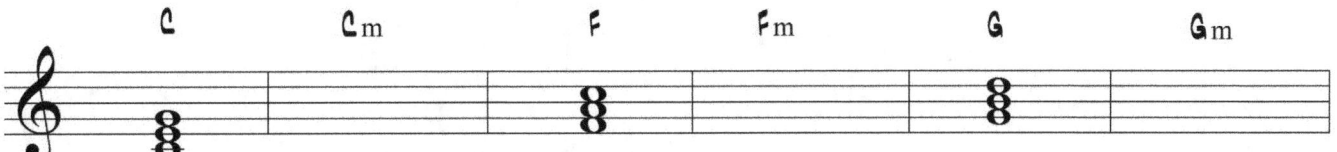

Worship at the Keys: A Method Book

The triads should look like this:

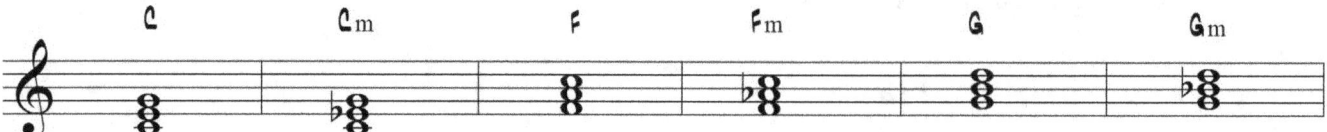

New Chords: Cm, Fm, Gm

Here is the list of triads you have already learned: C, D, Dm, Em, F, G, Am, Bm. Practice these in root position and inversions. Now add: Cm, Fm and Gm.

12-Bar Blues

The 12-bar blues sound even better when you add minor triads. The only difference between major and minor is the third, so use them both (one after the other, not at the same time) and see what happens. Some possible patterns for your right hand are:

Play the 12-bar blues using both major and minor triads in your right hand. Add the bass line with your left hand. The G chord at the end encourages you to repeat back to the beginning and keep playing.

12-Bar Blues Pattern #3

C	C	C	C
F	F	C	C
G	F	C	G

Unit 5: Playing Chord Charts

HUNT 'N PECK

Some melodies use notes that are not diatonic (not in the scale of the given key). In written music these notes show up as accidentals. Some of the melodies below have notes like this. Before you play each melody, play a chord progression you've learned for the given key and decide on a starting note for the melody.

Do-a-Deer (key of C)

O How I Love Jesus (key of C)

For He's a Jolly Good Fellow (The Bear Went Over the Mountain) (key of G)

Praise the Name of Jesus (play in the key of C)

O Little Town of Bethlehem (key of G)

Worship at the Keys: A Method Book

Unit 6: Flexibility

KEYBOARD STYLES

Step 1: Playing with a Worship Team

Playing with a worship team is very different from playing worship songs by yourself. You've already learned some techniques and styles for playing from lead sheets and chord charts. What you play will depend on what other instruments are in the band and what the worship leader wants. The "keys" player can fill many roles and your job is to have a servant's heart to play whatever is needed, but be bold. Confident playing sounds much better than timid playing. Here are some things to consider:

Is there a bass player?

No? You're the bass player! Play the bass line in a low octave and make it as interesting as you like.

Yes? You're not the bass player! You don't need to play the bass line at all, but if you do, play long notes in a higher bass clef octave and let the bass player have the fun.

Are there drums?

No? You and the guitar player (if there is one) are the rhythm section! Keep the beat going and play a quarter-note or other rhythm in your right hand. Don't stop or slow down when you make mistakes.

Yes? That's great! Your steady beat skills are going to improve every time you play along with drums. You aren't responsible for keeping the rhythm going – the song will go on no matter what you play, so don't stop to fix mistakes. Home practice with a metronome will help. You may be asked to play quarter notes or long sustained chords. If you're on a synthesizer, different sounds work better with different styles. Ask for suggestions or work it out with the worship leader.

Is there a guitar player?

No?   You're providing the harmony (the chords)! You will probably need to play right hand chords in the middle of the keyboard – around middle C. Quarter note rhythms may be better than whole notes.

Yes?   The guitar player will be playing the chords! You may be asked to play chords an octave higher, long notes instead of quarter notes, or fill in holes in the music with fragments of chords. You may not be ready for that, yet, so ask the worship leader what is best for you to play in your right hand. If the worship leader wants you to play the melody, ask if you can have a lead sheet.

Are you the only one playing an instrument?

No?   Good! It's fun to play with other people! Use the guidelines in this section and talk to the worship leader about what you should play.

Yes?   You get to be the bass section, the rhythm section and the harmony section! You will need all the techniques you've learned in previous chapters. Play a low bass line and keep a steady beat with quarter note chords, played in the middle of the keyboard. Play the last line of each song as an introduction and rehearse a lot with the worship leader.

Choruses, Verses and Bridges, Oh, My!

Worship songs may contain not only verse and chorus, but also an introduction, bridge, and maybe even a pre-chorus. These sections are usually marked on lead sheets and chord charts, but if they aren't, you can label them yourself. Worship leaders often jump from one section to another and they might not follow the order indicated in the music.

An advantage of chord charts over lead sheets is that everything usually fits on one page, which makes it easier to jump around. A disadvantage is that chords aren't always written over the right words. Make whatever notes you need on your music.

There is a complete chord chart of *Your Love Awakens Me* on page 57. Practice playing the sections out of order to build flexibility. Some worship leaders never sing a song the same way twice!

Chord Chart and Lead Sheet Services

There are online services where worship leaders can download chord charts and lead sheets. One of these is ccli.com. If your church or organization is a member of CCLI they should be able to print chord charts and lead sheets in any key. At first it may be easier for you to play from lead sheets, so if you are given chord charts and you'd really like lead sheets, you might want to ask. If your church does not subscribe to CCLI or something similar, suggest to your worship leader that they check it out!

Step 2: Practicing Being Flexible

Practice the chorus of *10,000 Reasons* trying each of the variations listed in Step 1. Imagine if you were playing with only a guitar player, or with guitar and drums, but no bass player, etc. Practice what you would play if you were the only instrumentalist. Notice how much you've learned since you started this book!

"10,000 Reasons" by Jonas Myrin and Matt Redman
Copyright © 2011 Thankyou Music (PRS) (adm. worldwide at CapitolCMGPublishing.com excluding Europe which is adm. by Integrity Music, part of the David C Cook family. Songs@integritymusic.com) / Atlas Mountain Songs (BMI) worshiptogether.com Songs (ASCAP) sixsteps Music (ASCAP) (adm. at CapitolCMGPublishing.com) All rights reserved. Used by permission.

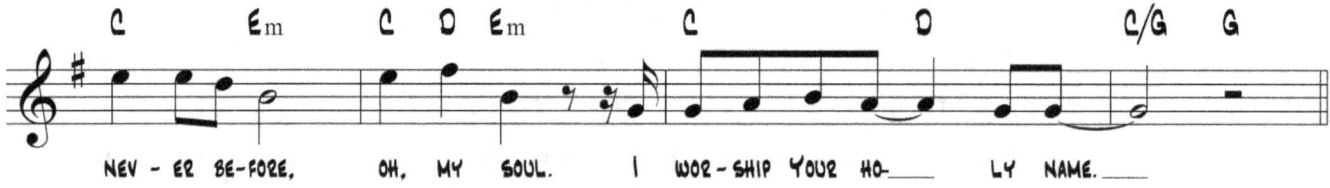

Step 3: Worship Song Practice

Practice the worship songs on the next few pages trying out different techniques. If you're already (or soon going to be) playing in a worship band, talk to the worship leader about what you should practice. If they tell you to do something differently than how you've learned in this book, do it their way.

10,000 Reasons

Words and music by
Jonas Myrin and Matt Redman

Bless the Lord, oh, my soul, oh, my soul. Wor-ship His ho- ly name. Sing like

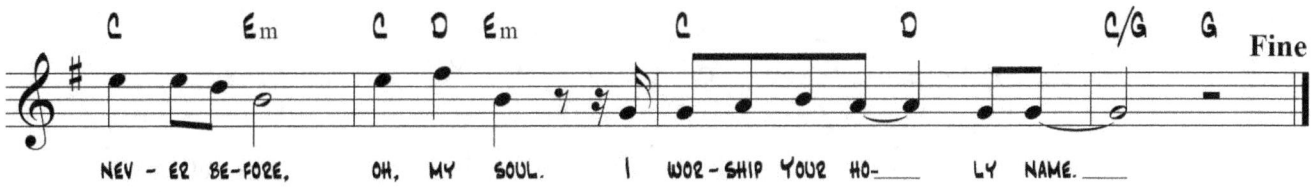
nev-er be-fore, oh, my soul. I wor-ship Your ho- ly name.

The sun comes up, it's a new day dawn-ing, it's time to sing Your song

a-gain. What-ev-er may pass, and what-ev-er lies be-fore me,

Let me be sing-ing when the eve-ning comes.

Copyright © 2011 Thankyou Music (PRS) (adm. worldwide at CapitolCMGPublishing.com excluding Europe which is adm. by Integrity Music, part of the David C Cook family. Songs@integritymusic.com) / Atlas Mountain Songs (BMI) worshiptogether.com Songs (ASCAP) sixsteps Music (ASCAP) (adm. at CapitolCMGPublishing.com)
All rights reserved. Used by permission.

This song uses a Gsus chord, which looks like this:
You can play Am for the Am7 chord.

My All in All

*Words and music by
Phil Wickham and Travis Ryan*

```
   C         F          Am7           G
You are my life,  You are my love,  You are my reason.

   C         F          Am7           G
You are my hope,  You are my joy,  You are my passion.

    F    C         Am7 G       F    C         Am7 G
My all in all,  Jesus my all in all    My all in all, Jesus my all in all.


     F       Am7           G
  In the desert You're the river,
 F         Am7            G
  An ever-flowing stream of life,
 F        Am7            G
  In the battle You're the victor
          F      C/E    G
And we raise Your banner high.
 F        Am7             G
  In the darkness You're the fire,
 F        Am7            G
  A holy flame for all to see,
 F           Am7              G
  And in my heart You reign forever,
      F    C/E  Gsus
My all, my ev'rything.
```

Copyright © 2011 Seems Like Music (BMI) / Phil Wickham Music (BMI)/Sing My Songs (BMI) All rights admin. by BMG
Rights Management c/o Music Services/Travis Ryan Music/Integrity Worship Music.
Copyright © 2015 Travis Ryan Music (ASCAP) Integrity Worship Music (ASCAP) (adm. at CapitolCMGPublishing.com) /Phil Wickham Music (BMI)
All rights reserved. Used by permission.

The slash marks (/) in the Intro indicate beats and the chord letter itself counts as one beat. The vertical lines (|) represent barlines. In this example there are six beats of G, two beats of Am, etc.

Your Love Awakens Me
Words and music by Phil Wickham and Chris Quilala

Intro (2x)
G / / / | / / Am / | C / / / | / / D / |

Verse 1
G
   There were walls between us, By the cross
               C
You came and broke them down,
You broke them down.
G
   There were chains around us, by Your grace
               C
we are no longer bound, no longer bound.

Pre-Chorus
D
   You called me out from the grave,
        Em   C
You called me into the light,
You called my name, and then
My heart came alive!

Chorus 1
G   C
   Your love is greater! Your love is stronger!
Em   D   C
   Your love awakens, awakens, awakens me!

Verse 2
G
   Feel the darkness shaking,
               C
All the dead are coming back to life,
I'm back to life.

G
   Hear the song awaken, all creation singing
C
We're alive, cause You're alive!

Pre-Chorus

Chorus 1

Bridge 1 (3x)
     C
And what a love we found!
G   Em
Death can't hold us down!
            D
Shout it out, "We're alive, cause You're alive!"

Chorus 2
G
   Your love is greater! Your love is stronger!
C
   Your love awakens, awakens, awakens me!

Chorus 3
G   Am
   Your love is greater! Your love is stronger!
Em   C   (G)
   Your love awakens, awakens, awakens me!

© 2016 Jesus Culture Music (ASCAP) Capitol CMG Genesis (ASCAP) (adm. at CapitolCMGPublishing.com) / Seems Like Music (BMI) / Phil Wickham Music (BMI) / Sing My Songs (BMI) All rights admin. by BMG Rights Management c/o Music Services/JESUS CULTURE (Capitol CMG Publishing).
All rights reserved. Used by permission.

Worship at the Keys: A Method Book

THEORY CORNER

As you gather a collection of lead sheets and chord charts you might see some unfamiliar chord symbols. There is a chart of chords in the back of this book that lists most of them. Start by memorizing the major and minor triads found most often in the songs you will be playing. The following sections explain how to play other types of chords you may encounter.

Major and Minor Triads

Guitar players prefer keys with sharps in the key signatures, so worship songs are often sung in sharp keys. Memorize the major and minor triads that you see in the songs your group sings. Here are the major triads you need to learn first. You already know a lot of them.

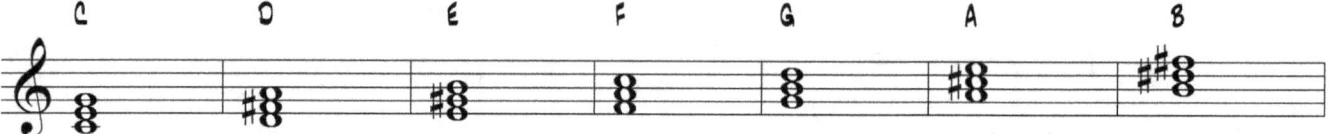

Here are minor triads that are helpful to know. There are just a few new ones.

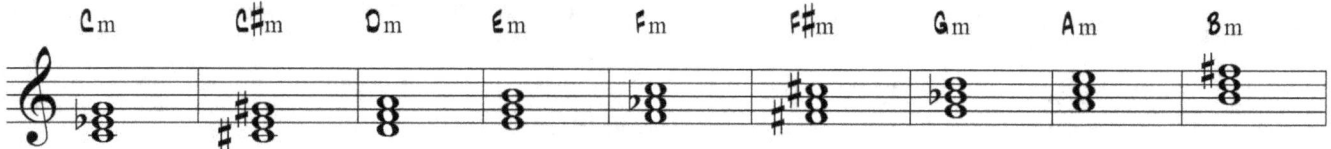

Practice new major and minor triads as needed, in root position and inversions.

Chords with Numbers

If you've looked at lead sheets or chord charts outside this book, you've probably seen chord symbols that have numbers in them, like C7 or Dm7. You may have seen chords like C2, C9 or C13. The numbers represent notes that are added to the triad. It's okay to ignore all numbers. If there is a lowercase "m" in the chord symbol, play the minor triad. If there is an uppercase "M," play the major triad. In some fonts a lowercase "m" looks like a small uppercase "M" (note the difference between **CM7** and **CM7**). Sorry.

If the chord symbol is: C2, C6, C7, CM7, Cmaj7, C9 or C13, play:

If the chord symbol is Cm7, Cmi7, Cmin7 or C-7, play:
Cmi, Cmin and C- are all ways of writing Cm.

When you're ready, look at the Chart of Chords on pages 70-71 and learn the extra notes in the chord. Adding the extra notes will make chords sound even better.

Sus Chords

Unlike chords with numbers, "sus" chords (suspended chords) can't be replaced with a major or minor triad. If you see Csus and you play C, it will clash with the other musicians. In a regular sus chord, the third is replaced with the fourth. In a sus2 chord, the third is replaced with the second. In a pinch, you can simply leave out the third of the triad.

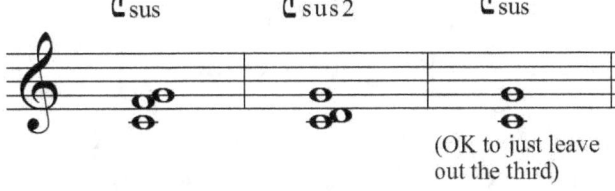

Sus chords are listed in the Chart of Chords. Memorize the ones you need.

Worship at the Keys: A Method Book

Diminished and Augmented Chords

Diminished triads (Cdim or C°) and augmented triads (Caug or C+) are not often found in today's worship music. Cdim is Cm with a lowered fifth. Caug is C with a raised fifth. These chords are also listed in the Chart of Chords.

Using New Chords

Below is a worship song that uses many different chords. Figure out how you would play each of these chords. Slash chords like Dm7/G are played with the Dm7 (or Dm) in your right hand and a "G" in your left hand. Get copies of worship songs you sing at your church and decide what chords you would use. Then, practice the songs.

Jesus, Lover of My Soul

Words and music by
Daniel Grul, John Ezzy and Steve McPherson

```
C        Bm7         Am/E    Eaug
  Jesus, lover of my soul,

Am7         Dm7         Dm7/G
  Jesus, I will never let You go.

C             Bm7         Am/E    Eaug
  You've taken me from the miry clay,

Am7             Dm7         Dm7/G
  Set my feet upon the rock and now I know,

C        G/B        Am        Gm7      C7      F
  I love You,  I need You,   Though my world may fall, I'll never let You go.

C        G/B        Am        Gm7      FM7
  My Savior,  my closest friend,  I will worship You until the very end.
```

Copyright © 2000 Hillsong Music Publishing (APRA) (adm. in the US and Canada at CapitolCMGPublishing.com) All rights reserved. Used by permission.

HUNT 'N PECK

You can add bass notes to the melodies you play by ear. First, figure out how to play the melody of each song with your right hand. Then, add a bass line with your left hand using the the given notes where they sound best.

London Bridge (play in key of C, add bass notes C, G)

Mary Had a Little Lamb (play in key of G, add bass notes G, D)

God is So Good (play in key of C, add bass notes C, F and G)

Kum Ba Yah (play in key of G, add bass notes G, C and D)

Jingle Bells (play in key of C, add bass notes C, D, F and G)

Worship at the Keys: A Method Book

Unit 7: Playing in New Keys

KEYBOARD STYLES

Step 1: Learning Songs in a New Key: D

As you branch out to songs in new keys, your first task is to become familiar with the scale and chords you need to play in that key. You can look through the lead sheet to find any chords you don't already know. Here is the D major scale:

Looking at worship songs written in the key of D Major, you will probably see the chords below. Practice them in root position and inversions.

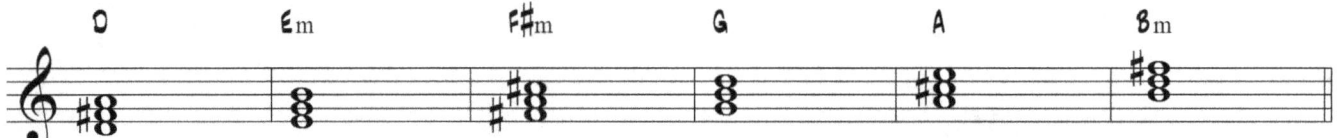

Step 2: Practice Chord Progressions

If this is your first time playing in the new key, it is also helpful to learn some chord progressions. These chord progressions are the same ones you've seen before in the keys of C and G, but they have been transposed to the key of D. Practice until you can play them smoothly using root position and inversions in your right hand and a bass line in your left hand.

Progression #1:   D   G   D   A   D

Progression #2:   F#m   Bm   Em   A   D

Step 3: Worship Song Practice

Play as many songs as you can find in the new key. Playing in the new key will become easier the more you do it. On the next pages are songs to get you started in the key of D. If you don't already know the song, listen to a recording until it is familiar. Get copies of songs your group sings in the key of D and practice them, too.

Copyright © 2010 Thankyou Music (PRS) (adm. worldwide at CapitolCMGPublishing.com excluding Europe which is adm. by Integrity Music, part of the David C Cook family. Songs@integritymusic.com / Atlas Mountain Songs (BMI) worshiptogether.com Songs (ASCAP) Vamos Publishing (ASCAP) sixsteps Music (ASCAP) (adm. at CapitolCMGPublishing.com) All rights reserved. Used by permission.

Open the Eyes of My Heart

Words and music by Paul Baloche

Copyright © 1997 Integrity's Hosanna! Music (ASCAP) (adm. at CapitolCMGPublishing.com) All rights reserved. Used by permission.

You Are My King (Amazing Love)

Words and music by
Billy James Foote

Verse
D/F#   G   A
  I'm forgiven because You were forsaken.
D/F#   G   A
  I'm accepted, You were condemned.
D/F# G   A
  I'm alive and well, Your Spirit is within me
     G   A   D
Because You died and rose again.

Chorus
D   G
  Amazing love, how can it be
D   A   G/A
  That You my King, would die for me?
D   G
  Amazing love, I know it's true;
D   A
  It's my joy to honor You.
       G A   D
In all I do,   I honor You.

Bridge
D
You are my King, You are my King.
Jesus, You are my King, You are my King.

Copyright © 1999 worshiptogether.com Songs (ASCAP) (adm. at CapitolCMGPublishing.com)
All rights reserved. Used by permission.

Oceans (Where Feet May Fail)

Words and music by
Joel Houston, Matt Crocker and Salomon Ligthelm

Verse

Bm   A/C#   D
You call me out upon the waters,

            A   G
The great unknown where feet may fail.

Bm   A/C# D
And there I find You in the mystery,

      A   G
In oceans deep, my faith will stand.

Chorus

G   D   A
And I will call upon Your name

G   D   A
And keep my eyes above the waves.

       G   D   A
When oceans rise, my soul will rest in Your embrace

     G   A   Bm
For I am Yours and You are mine.

Copyright © 2013 Hillsong Music Publishing (APRA) (adm. in the US and Canada at CapitolCMGPublishing.com)
All rights reserved. Used by permission.

THEORY CORNER

Transposing

Here is a transposition chart with the key of D major added. There is a full chart on page 72 that includes all the major keys.

Key	Key Sig.	I	ii	iii	IV	V	vi
C	nothing	C	Dm	Em	F	G	Am
G	F#	G	Am	Bm	C	D	Em
D	F#, C#	D	Em	F#m	G	A	Bm

You can use this chart to transpose any of the songs in C to the key of D. Here is the chorus of *Holy Spirit* in C.

"Holy Spirit" by Bryan Torwalt and Katie Torwalt
Copyright © 2011 Capitol CMG Genesis (ASCAP) Jesus Culture Music (ASCAP)
(adm. at CapitolCMGPublishing.com) All rights reserved. Used by permission.

```
C                              Am/F            Dm
Holy Spirit, You are welcome here:  Come flood this place and fill the atmosphere.

    C                                    Am/F          Dm         C
Your glory, God, is what our hearts long for,  To be overcome by Your presence, Lord.
```

You can transpose *Holy Spirit* to the key of D. On the slash chords, follow the letters in the columns to determine the bass. The first two chords are done for you. Transpose the rest to the key of D. Check your work by playing the song.

```
D                              Bm/G
Holy Spirit, You are welcome here:  Come flood this place and fill the atmosphere.


Your glory, God, is what our hearts long for,  To be overcome by Your presence, Lord.
```

Worship at the Keys: A Method Book

Improvising in D

Below is a chord progression in the key of D. Play it using right hand triads in root position and inversions. Each chord gets four beats. Add a simple bass line.

D A Bm F#m G D G A (repeat)

Now try the same chord progression, but play the chord inversions so the note written in the treble clef in the example below is the top note of your chord.

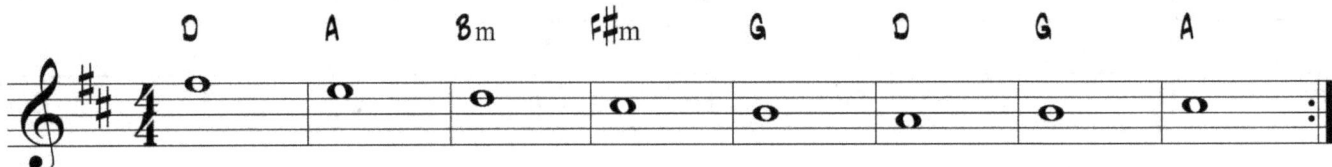

Does it sound familiar? This is the chord progression used in Pachelbel's *Canon in D*. Try it again playing some chord notes individually. You can play whatever you want to make it pretty, just remember to keep a steady beat. Here is one way to get started:

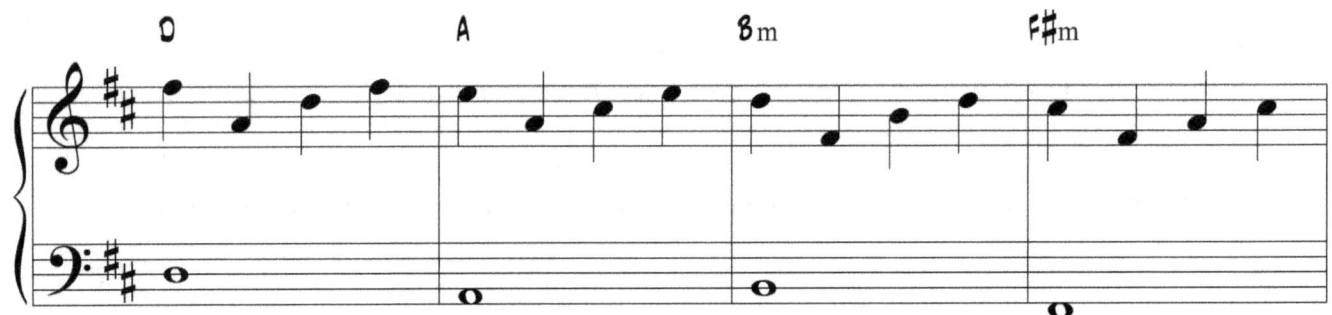

If you'd rather play Pachelbel in the key of C, transpose it here:

Key D: D A Bm F#m G D G A (repeat)

Key C:

Unit 7: Playing in New Keys

HUNT 'N PECK

Find melodies by ear in the key of D. Before you play each melody, play one of these chord progressions. Notice how much easier it is, now, to play by ear than it was when you started this book!

> Progression #1: D   G   D   A   D
>
> Progression #2: F#m   Bm   Em   A   D

Row, Row, Row Your Boat
Twinkle, Twinkle Little Star
Mary Had a Little Lamb
London Bridge
Yankee Doodle
Old MacDonald
Pop! Goes the Weasel
Amazing Grace
Jingle Bells

Worship at the Keys: A Method Book

Chart of Chords

Lead sheet chord symbols can be written different ways. The most common variations are listed along with each type of chord.

Major Triads: C, CM, C△

Minor Triads: Cm, Cmi, Cmin, C_M, C-

Diminished Triads: Cdim, C°

Augmented Triads: Caug, C+

Major Triad with Added 2nd: C2, (C9 is often played like C2 in church and pop music)

Major Triad with no 3rd: C5, C(no 3rd)

Suspended Triads: Here are two kinds: Csus (same as Csus4) and Csus2

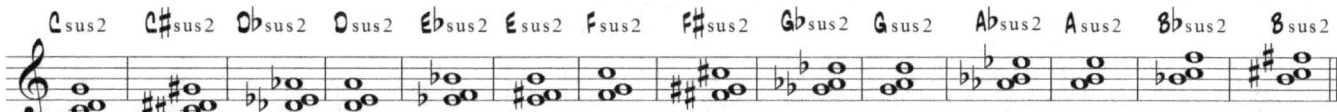

Major Seventh Chords: CM7, Cmaj7, C△7

Dominant Seventh Chords: C7

Minor Seventh Chords: Cm7, Cmi7, Cmin7, CM7, C-7

Half-diminished Seventh Chords: Cm7(b5), Cm7b5, Cø7

Diminished Seventh Chords: Cdim7, C°7

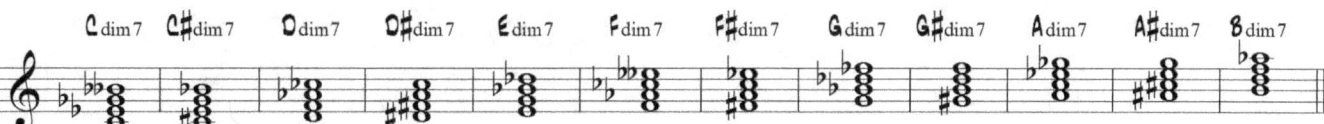

Worship at the Keys: A Method Book

Transposition Chart

Key	Key Sig.	I	ii	iii	IV	V	vi
C	none	C	Dm	Em	F	G	Am
G	F#	G	Am	Bm	C	D	Em
D	F#, C#	D	Em	F#m	G	A	Bm
A	F#, C#, G#	A	Bm	C#m	D	E	F#m
E	F#, C#, G#, D#	E	F#m	G#m	A	B	C#m
B	F#, C#, G#, D#, A#	B	C#m	D#m	E	F#	G#m
F#	F#, C#, G#, D#, A#, E#	F#	G#m	A#m	B	C#	D#m
C#	F#, C#, G#, D#, A#, E#, B#	C#	D#m	E#m	F#	G#	A#m
F	Bb	F	Gm	Am	Bb	C	Dm
Bb	Bb, Eb	Bb	Cm	Dm	Eb	F	Gm
Eb	Bb, Eb, Ab	Eb	Fm	Gm	Ab	Bb	Cm
Ab	Bb, Eb, Ab, Db	Ab	Bbm	Cm	Db	Eb	Fm
Db	Bb, Eb, Ab, Db, Gb	Db	Ebm	Fm	Gb	Ab	Bbm
Gb	Bb, Eb, Ab, Db, Gb, Cb	Gb	Abm	Bbm	Cb	Db	Ebm
Cb	Bb, Eb, Ab, Db, Gb, Cb, Fb	Cb	Dbm	Ebm	Fb	Gb	Abm

About the Author

Donna Gielow McFarland started playing the piano by hunting and pecking the melody of *Do-a-Deer* when she was eight. In middle school she taught herself how to play worship songs from chord charts and in college she wrote her masters project on how classically trained pianists can learn to improvise for playing in church.

After receiving a B.Mus. in Piano Performance from Wheaton College and an M.Mus. in Piano Pedagogy from the University of Oregon, Donna taught a number of courses including piano, class piano, music theory and ear training at New Hope Christian College and, currently, Northwest Christian University. Donna has published eight music books including *Follow the Star: Christmas Songs for Piano (Vol. 1-5)*, *Intro to Piano: Class Piano for Adult Beginners* and *Music Theory Made Simpl(er)*. She has also written several children's early readers and chapter books. Donna lives in Eugene, Oregon with her husband and son.

About the Illustrator

Jack Foster lives near Chicago with his wife Aleithia and their cat, Jasper. He is a husband to one, a father to five and a grandfather to 14. He is a follower of Jesus, a children's book illustrator and a mailman. He is a Sunday school teacher at his church. He has illustrated over 60 books and he has fun with the boys and girls on his mail route. He likes to give books away to the children of his customers.